RESET: FATHERHOOD EDITION

A 21-DAY DEVOTIONAL FOR FATHERS

Dr. Barry Settle

First edition published June 2024

ISBN: 9798328137164

DEDICATION

This 21-day devotional is dedicated to my father, Willie Settle. As of this writing, he is 92 years old. I could not have asked God for a better father, a man who was present both physically and emotionally all of my life.

Also, to my older brother, Stanley Settle, who was married and a father by the time I was 19 years old. He became a more contemporary model of fatherhood for me as a young adult.

There are others I need to mention. What I have learned is that no one fathers alone. I was fortunate growing up to have a village of fathers who aided in my rearing up until I became a young adult. From the age of four, I grew up with my friends and their fathers, as well as the other fathers in our neighborhood, who fathered me and aided in my development. I remembered them as well as I wrote this devotional. Jake LaRue, Ronald McCauley, Donald Jones, William Shumate, Charles Hoskins, Bennie Townsend and O'Dell Ross.

To my father in ministry, Rev. Norman D. Copeland.

To my friends who are fathers, too many to mention. You inspire me.

Finally, to every father who is doing the best they can to be a great father, this devotional is for you.

Table of Contents

INTRODUCTION

Merriam-Webster Dictionary defines the word "reset" as follows: "to set again or anew."

Collins English Dictionary says, "If you reset a machine or device, you adjust or set it, so that it is ready to work again or ready to perform a particular function."

This is a new edition of RESET, specifically tailored for fathers.

Fathers and stepfathers, God has entrusted children to your care. Regardless of whether they are your biological child or stepchild, they need you as their father.

Fathers, we need to reset. We need to adjust spiritually so that we are ready to function and live in a way that pleases God. If we fail to reset from time to time, we can fall into a place of complacency, where we are satisfied with where we are spiritually, failing to grow closer to God because we are content with mediocrity.

Being a father is a tough job. As a father and working for years with men, many of whom are fathers, I hear firsthand their feelings regarding being a father, including those about the lack of support that is available specifically for fathers. In a society that can be dismissive of the role of fathers, this devotional is written specifically for you. You are appreciated, valued, and needed in society. It is God who has given us the privilege to be fathers, and we should be grateful for that.

This 21-day devotion is to help us reset our lives, to take time and reflect on us as fathers. I am calling you to be open and honest with yourself about your spiritual and parental life. It may be uncomfortable, but you will benefit from your attempt to reset in this manner.

As in my original edition of RESET, I left space for personal reflection. In RESET: FATHER'S EDITION, at the end of each devotion, there are questions that you are asked to reflect on. As you reflect, write down your honest answers. RESET: FATHER'S EDITION is intended to be read in the morning before you start your day. I would suggest waking up twenty to thirty minutes earlier than usual, getting your coffee or tea, and prayerfully diving into this RESET. This will give you time to read, digest, and reflect on each day's devotion.

Fathers, my prayer is that this devotional blesses your life, helps you to reflect on becoming a better father, and aids in your spiritual growth. As you reset your life over the next 21 days, I suggest you also apply the following spiritual disciplines.

Prayer – Prayer should be a part of our daily walk with Christ. For the next 21 days, commit yourself to spending twice the amount of time you normally would in prayer each day. For example, if you normally spend ten minutes daily, for the next 21 days, spend twenty minutes daily in prayer.

Study – In addition to these devotionals, read your Bible daily. Read 1-2 chapters daily. Per day. Read slowly, not taking for granted that you may be familiar with the scriptures. Reflect, re-read, highlight, and meditate on what you are reading daily.

Quiet Solitude – For many, our days are filled with endless demands and noise. Sometimes, we need to be quiet and still to hear from God. The psalmist writes, "Be still, and know I am God. I will be exalted among the nations, I will be exalted in the earth" (Ps. 46:10). Turn off the television, close your laptop, put your phone down. Let us spend extended periods of quiet solitude before God each day.

Fasting – Fast at least once a week over the next 21 days. If you are not used to fasting, fast for one meal during the day. If fasting is a regular spiritual discipline that you practice, fast from 6 a.m. to 6 p.m., where you drink only water/juice/tea (only engage in a fast if you are physically able—check with your physician if you are concerned).

Worship – Commit to attending worship every Sunday during these 21 days.

All scriptures are from the Christian Standard Bible (CSB) unless otherwise noted.

Fathers, let us begin our RESET.

DAY 1

But if it doesn't please you to worship the Lord, choose
for yourselves today: Which will you worship—the gods
your ancestors worshiped beyond the Euphrates River or
the gods of the Amorites in whose land you are living?
As for me and my family, we will worship the Lord."
Joshua 24:15

The first lesson of fatherhood is to reset ourselves to God. Fatherhood is a selfless responsibility, and we are not capable of being effective fathers to our children unless we ourselves have reset ourselves with our Lord. As we father our children, it should be clear to them that we love and serve God with all of our heart, mind, and soul. This is not to suggest that we go out of our way to ensure our children see us studying our Bibles, praying, attending worship, and loving humanity. However, if our children are not witnesses to this as our consistent lifestyle, perhaps this has not been a priority in our lives. Every father could use a RESET in their relationship with God. Fatherhood is difficult enough, and we will need an active and consistent relationship with the Lord in order to grow and develop as fathers.

Just as two choices were presented to the people in the text, Joshua models excellent leadership by making the declaration that regardless of other choices, for him and his household, serving God will be a priority. Fathers, let us make this commitment for our homes.

Prayer – *Lord, today I seek to make sure that as I reset myself to the commitment to be a father to my children, by putting you first in my life. Help me to align my life accordingly, making you my ultimate priority in my life. Please give me that desire. In Jesus' name, Amen.*

Reflection Questions

Reflect and brainstorm on intentional ways that you can reset your relationship with God.

_____

_____

_____

_____

_____

_____

_____

_____

_____

_____

_____

_____

_____

_____

_____

_____

_____

_____

_____

_____

List the obstacles present in your life that prevent you from making God your daily priority. Once you identify them, develop a routine that will eliminate the obstacles.

_____

_____

_____

_____

_____

_____

_____

_____

_____

_____

_____

_____

_____

_____

_____

_____

_____

_____

DAY 2

Enjoy life with the wife you love all the days of your fleeting life, which has been given to you under the sun, all your fleeting days. For that is your portion in life and in your struggle under the sun.
Ecclesiastes 9:9

One of the greatest lessons fatherhood teaches our children is the way we love and respect our wives. Loving and respecting our wives teaches our sons how to treat women, and it teaches our daughters how they should expect to be treated by men. Fathers, loving and respecting the mother of our children is a critical component of fatherhood. Let us consider a RESET on how we live with our wives. In this text, Solomon speaks of us enjoying our wives with all the remaining days of mercy we receive from God. Marriage was instituted by God in the Garden, as found in Genesis 2:24, and Jesus also addressed marriage in Matthew 19:4-6. Both of these scripture texts reference the man and woman becoming one flesh, which I often refer to as the journey of oneness. Let us move in this manner, honoring God by loving, cherishing, and serving our wives.

Of course, we understand that in our society, things happen where we, as fathers, may not be married to the mother of our children for many reasons. This does not absolve us from treating the mother of our children respectfully with kindness and grace. What a gift for our children to witness their father behave in this manner!

Prayer – *Lord, today I want to work on treating the mother of my children with the respect they deserve. Regardless of the complexities of the relationship, help me with your Holy Spirit to always be mindful of this, showing my children how women should be honored and respected. In Jesus' name, Amen.*

Reflection Questions

Prayerfully consider how you can show respect to the mother of your children and ways you can improve making this attribute consistent in your daily life.

_____

_____

_____

_____

_____

_____

_____

_____

_____

_____

_____

_____

_____

_____

_____

_____

Depending on your circumstances, consider practical ways you can show more love and respect to your wife that you will put into practice today. If you are not married to the mother of your children, consider practical ways you can still show kindness and respect when you two interact.

_____

_____

_____

_____

_____

_____

_____

_____

_____

_____

_____

_____

_____

_____

DAY 3

Train up a child in the way he should go; even when he is old he will not depart from it.
Proverbs 22:6 English Standard Version

Merriam-Webster defines "train" as to teach so as to make fit, qualified, or proficient; or to direct the growth of, usually by bending, pruning, and tying. Fathers, this is our calling—to train and direct our children. One effective way to train them is by example. If we instruct our children on how to act and behave but then live in a contradictory manner, it undermines everything we try to teach them.

Let us live as examples in their presence, serving the Lord and showing respect and honor for their mother as we teach and guide them alongside their mother. This process works so much better when fathers and mothers are united in this effort. When mistakes are made by you as a father, explain the errors to your children so they can learn as well from your mistakes. None of us is perfect, and as I reflect on my own father, I learned not only from his strengths but also from his mistakes. We should not be led to feel as if we need to be without fault as we strive to train our children. Authenticity is an amazing lesson in itself.

Prayer – *Lord, help me today to live up to the standards I attempt to teach my children, so they do not see any contradiction between my words and my conduct. In your Son Jesus' name, Amen.*

Reflection Questions

Reflect on your life and consider the spaces in it where your children may see a contraction between your words and your actions. What will you do to correct this?

_____

_____

_____

_____

_____

_____

_____

_____

_____

_____

_____

_____

_____

_____

_____

_____

What are some godly characteristics that I would love to teach and show my children to help them in their development? It could be tithing, trusting in God, walking in obedience/faith, forgiveness, etc.

DAY 4

*Grandchildren are the crown of the elderly, and
the pride of children is their fathers.
Proverbs 17:6*

…and the pride of children is their fathers.

Fathers, you matter! You are important and critical to the lives of your children. This is not to discredit mothers or the place of mothers in the lives of the children, but to you fathers, know how valued you are to your sons and daughters. In our society, we do not do a good enough job of celebrating the fathers and men who have taken on the role of fathers in the lives of their children. You are critical in the development of your children to fulfill the potential God has for them in their lives. Do not allow any circumstance to convince you otherwise. This text reveals an adult child with his/her child, perhaps in the presence of the adult child's father. It is perhaps a moment when the adult child, now a parent, appreciates and respects the role of the father in their life. No words may need to be communicated, but there is perhaps just a realization of all the father was to this now adult child, and the adult child is grateful and proud of the father God allowed him/her to have. Here is where you are crowned with grandchildren and appreciated by your family, all for being obedient to the calling of God to be a father.

Fathers, thank you for being a father to your child.

Prayer – *Lord, today my prayer is to ask you to help me to be the best father possible to my children. Give me patience and wisdom as I do all I can today. In Jesus' name, Amen.*

Reflection Questions

How can you personally counteract the narrative of society's view of fathers within your family and community?

_____

_____

_____

_____

_____

_____

_____

_____

_____

_____

_____

_____

_____

_____

_____

_____

_____

Consider how you can celebrate and appreciate the role of fathers in your community. How will you intentionally encourage the fathers you interact with?

_____

_____

_____

_____

_____

_____

_____

_____

_____

_____

_____

_____

_____

_____

_____

_____

DAY 5

Then they sat on the ground with him seven days and nights, but no one spoke a word to him because they saw that his suffering was very intense.
Job 2:13

As a father, you will wear many different hats. Counselor, disciplinarian, teacher, and numerous others. One hat you will also have to wear is that of a friend. There are times when you will need to be your children's friend. This term's definition has changed in the last decade with the popularity of social media, but Merriam-Webster defines a friend as "one attached to another by affection or esteem." It implies that one cares for the other deeply and wants what is best for that person. There are times when our children will need their father to be their friend. Times when circumstances in their lives dictate that they need someone they can trust and depend on to be a friend. Our children will need us to be there for them. Here in the text, although this is not referring to a father/child relationship, it does demonstrate friends being present in the need of another friend. What is significant in the story of Job and his friends here is that

17

they were present with him for seven days, not providing any input, suggestions, or advice to Job's predicament. They were present and they listened because that is what their friend needed.

Fathers, there will be times when you, being present and listening—not trying to solve your child's problem—will be exactly what they need in their father. Being a trusted friend who is also their father.

Prayer – *Lord, give me the discernment to know when my child needs me to be their friend and give me the strength to move into that space willingly. In Jesus' name, Amen.*

Reflection Questions

What circumstances are there in your children's lives where they can possibly be looking for their father to be a trusted friend?

_____

_____

_____

_____

_____

_____

_____

_____

_____

_____

_____

_____

_____

_____

_____

How will you balance being a father and a friend to your children?

_____

_____

_____

_____

_____

_____

_____

_____

_____

_____

_____

_____

_____

_____

_____

_____

_____

_____

_____

DAY 6

And you saw in the wilderness how the LORD your God carried you as a man carries his son all along the way you traveled until you reached this place.
Deuteronomy 1:31

One of the things I have learned is that fatherhood does not end when your children turn eighteen, but rather, this is just the beginning. When our children become adults, they begin to push for their own independence, often with their own struggles and difficulties. Some reach this place quicker than others; however, we are still fathers to our children in the process. It never ends.

God always fought on behalf of Israel, even in the desert. Today's text says the Lord carried Israel, as a father carries his child, and a father carries that child all the way. This demonstrates a faithful and compassionate God who never gives up on us and is with us forever. Fathers, remember our children will have wilderness seasons in their lives, and they need us to be the fathers who will walk with them until they reach their desired place in life. Let us prepare to walk with our children with compassionate support for a lifetime. This will look different in each of our contexts, but it could look like periodically sharing a meal with your son/daughter just to hear what is going on in their lives. It could also look like a "like" on their latest accomplishment on social media. Support takes many different forms. May this give us insight on what they are dealing with personally as it guides our prayers for them.

Prayer – Lord, thank you for my children, and I ask you to please provide me with what I need to be a constant presence in their lives. Give me the discernment of when to be silent, when to offer advice, and when to encourage. In Jesus' name, Amen.

Reflection Questions

How will you support your children as they continue to strive for independence?

_____

_____

_____

_____

_____

_____

_____

_____

_____

_____

_____

_____

_____

_____

_____

_____

_____

_____

_____

Consider wilderness experiences your children are currently experiencing. How will you show compassionate support to them?

_____

_____

_____

_____

_____

_____

_____

_____

_____

_____

_____

_____

_____

_____

_____

_____

_____

_____

DAY 7

In the fear of the Lord one has strong confidence and his children have a refuge.
Proverbs 14:26

Fathers, let us embrace a fear of the Lord along with the benefits of this fear, not only for us but for our children as well. Our fear of God gives us the confidence that He is a shelter and refuge for us as we journey through the storms of fatherhood and maintain obedience to God and His ways. This is a powerful example for our children to see. They see the benefit of fearing God.

Fathers who fear the Lord understand that God has placed our children under our care and that they should be guided and shaped by our decisions until they reach the age at which they can make choices for themselves. We are responsible to model and teach our children to fear God as we model it for them. We allow the Holy Spirit to guide us as fathers, shaping our children through guidance, advice, and instruction.

During the seasons of our children's lives, they will face numerous influences
from friends, social media, and society. It is critical to demonstrate a fear of God as early and consistently as we can. This may not always be popular with our children, but it's essential for them to see us, as fathers, display this in our lives.

Prayer – *God, my prayer today is that because of my fear of you, I will conform my will to your will, with the confidence that you will help me become a better father. In Jesus' name, Amen.*

Reflection Questions

How does your fear of God impact your confidence as a father?

_____

_____

_____

_____

_____

_____

_____

_____

_____

_____

_____

_____

_____

_____

_____

_____

_____

Consider the variety of influences your children are currently dealing with and reflect on how your example of fearing God offsets those influences. Write your thoughts.

_____

_____

_____

_____

_____

_____

_____

_____

_____

_____

_____

_____

_____

_____

_____

DAY 8

Fathers, don't stir up anger in your children, but bring them up in the training and instruction of the Lord.
Ephesians 6:4

As fathers, we are called to take heart the instructions in this verse. A similar message in Colossians 3:21 says, "Fathers, do not exasperate your children, so that they won't become discouraged." Both scriptures emphasize how we should approach disciplining our children.

Discipline is essential in raising our sons and daughters, but it should not ever be abusive or discouraging. We must exercise godly self-control and discernment, ensuring our correction can have a powerful effect and, at the same time, display fatherly love. We do not want our discipline to provoke anger or resentment. Our goal is that discipline will guide and improve our children's growth and development with the purpose of building our children up (not tearing them down) and helping them mature personally, emotionally, and spiritually. We want to not only correct behavior but also develop their godly character. Let us remember that we are their role model, so again, they learn from what we model before them. When we discipline, we are investing in their development into becoming the persons God desires. The balance of this approach can create a healthy relationship between fathers and their children.

Prayer – *God, my prayer is that you help me discern ways to discipline my children that will correct their behavior when necessary while at the same time developing them spiritually. Help me to exercise self-control whenever I discipline them. In Jesus' name, Amen.*

Reflection Questions

Reflect on how you discipline your children. What areas do you believe you need to exercise more self-control?

_____

_____

_____

_____

_____

_____

_____

_____

_____

_____

_____

_____

_____

_____

_____

_____

Consider other methods of discipline that effectively balance correction with building your children up emotionally and spiritually. Write out how you will improve your discipline to include "building up."

_____

_____

_____

_____

_____

_____

_____

_____

_____

_____

_____

_____

_____

_____

_____

_____

DAY 9

Rejoice in hope, be patient in affliction, be persistent in
prayer
Romans 12:12

Rejoicing hope, patience in affliction. This combination of hope and affliction drives us to our knees in prayer. As fathers, we are filled with the hope and expectation that our children will live up to the great potential we see in them. We constantly affirm our children and the gifts God has blessed them with. And with this comes the normal trouble that occurs in their lives, as life has its own way of draining our children of the expectant hope we have for them. As we wrestle with this, we are reminded to keep prayer as a great discipline in our lives, involving God to intervene in our children's lives and direct them in the way they should go. The scripture urges us to "keep on praying," which lets us know, as fathers, that we should constantly pray for our children. Pray for them daily and as often as you think of them throughout your day. Rejoicing in hope, patience in affliction, and persistent prayer will support our children throughout the trials in their lives. As we apply the tools from this devotional, involving ourselves in the lives of our children, ask God to show you ways that you can pray daily for your sons and daughters.

Prayer – *Lord, I lift my children up to you now in the name of Jesus. Encourage them by your Holy Spirit in any struggle they are currently facing. In Jesus' name, Amen*

Reflection Questions

Ask your children this morning about any trouble they are experiencing currently so you can know how you can pray for them daily. List them here, and focus on making prayer an integral part of your daily discipline.

_____

_____

_____

_____

_____

_____

_____

_____

_____

_____

_____

_____

_____

_____

_____

Reflect on the hope that is involved in being a father. How will you instill this hope in your children?

_____

_____

_____

_____

_____

_____

_____

_____

_____

_____

_____

_____

_____

_____

_____

_____

_____

_____

DAY 10

As a father has compassion on his children, so the Lord has
compassion on those who fear him.
Psalm 103:13

The word "compassion" in Hebrew describes a mother caring for a vulnerable or weak child. It suggests being deeply moved, implying action should be taken. Our children need faithful fathers who are deeply moved by the experiences they deal with in life. Let our attention to being compassionate be a reliable characteristic of our fatherhood. This may require vulnerability on our part to feel the pains of our children's lives like they are our pains. When our children hurt, we should hurt, as well as be willing to move into these emotional spaces with them.

As God is compassionate toward us, we should show this same compassion toward our children. One way to demonstrate this is by listening intently and moving accordingly toward what we hear our children communicating to us, even if that means offering no advice.

As compassionate fathers we should strive to put ourselves in our children's shoes and provide for them what they need in these moments, rather than focusing on what we want them to learn or understand. As we personify this compassionate approach, we mirror God's care and develop a nurturing environment where our children are supported and understood.

Prayer – *Lord, I thank you for how compassionate you are toward me; please allow me to show the same compassionate love toward my children. In Jesus' name, Amen.*

Reflection Questions

Reflect on a time when your child needed you to be compassionate toward them. What was your response, and what would you do differently in that circumstance if you could?

_____

_____

_____

_____

_____

_____

_____

_____

_____

_____

_____

_____

_____

_____

What are some practical things that you could equip yourself to better empathize with your children's experience?

_____

_____

_____

_____

_____

_____

_____

_____

_____

_____

_____

_____

_____

_____

_____

_____

_____

DAY 11

*I will instruct you and show you the way to go; with my eye on you,
I will give counsel
Psalm 32:8*

One extraordinary quality of God is the reliable provision of clear instructions and guidance for us, His children. God not only instructs us but also demonstrates these teachings through His Son, Jesus Christ. Jesus's life was a perfect expression of God's instructions. As fathers, our guidance for our children should reflect God's approach, combining instruction with demonstration. Fathers, our lives should serve as a living example of the values and principles we teach our sons and daughters. It is imperative that there is no inconsistency between our words and our actions. Let our conduct consistently reinforce the lessons we impart, ensuring that our children see a harmonious alignment between what we say and what we do. This alignment will help instill in them the values we hold dear and the guidance we believe to be true. As fathers, let us strive to be the embodiment of the instruction we give, just as Jesus was for

41

God's teachings. Our ultimate goal as fathers is to live in a way that exemplifies the principles we want our children to adopt and follow throughout their lives. If we live by the instructions we provide for them, they are likely to understand the importance of these life lessons.

Prayer – *Lord, today give me discernment to hear your instructions and the courage to follow you. Give me ears to hear your counsel as my Heavenly Father. In Jesus' name, Amen.*

Reflection Questions

How are you seeking God's instructions and guidance in your life as a father? What are your disciplines?

_____

_____

_____

_____

_____

_____

_____

_____

_____

_____

_____

_____

_____

_____

_____

_____

What are you doing to be a constant example of the values that you teach your children?

_____

_____

_____

_____

_____

_____

_____

_____

_____

_____

_____

_____

_____

_____

_____

_____

DAY 12

Love is patient, love is kind. Love does not envy, is not boastful,
is not arrogant, is not rude, is not self-seeking, is not irritable,
and does not keep a record of wrongs.
1 Corinthians 13:4-5

The love a father has for his children is one that cannot be described by words alone. Nothing can replace this unwavering, deep affection between a father and his child. Therefore, it is crucial for fathers to remember the biblical definition of love outlined in 1 Corinthians 13. It defines all the attributes of what love means. One critical quality found in v. 5b is love does not keep a record of wrongs. As fathers become frustrated during the process of fathering, it can be easy to call to mind all the mistakes our children make and remind them of these occurrences. However, fatherly love demands that we release and let go of these records. Reminding our children of every mistake in the process of fathering can discourage them and damage their sense of self-worth. Our love as fathers should move us to forgive and focus on how our children can continue to develop and grow.

If embracing 1 Corinthians 13 as our model for fatherly love, God constructs for us the ability to engage our children with patience and kindness, crafting a space where our children can thrive and at the same time feel secure to grow from mistakes without the fear of being reminded of them. This love builds the relationship between the father and child and at the same time teaches the child how God loves, as well.

Prayer – *Heavenly Father, please teach me how to love my children in the same manner that you love me. Help to erase the record of wrongs, that I have kept on file on my children. In Jesus' name, Amen.*

Reflection Questions

List the records of wrongs you are keeping on our children. Pray and ask God to help you erase this list in your heart, never to bring them up again to your children.

_____

_____

_____

_____

_____

_____

_____

_____

_____

_____

_____

_____

_____

_____

_____

_____

_____

Prayerfully ask God to soften your heart so that you will not list any more mistakes to bring up in the future and to give you a new heart toward your children.

_____

_____

_____

_____

_____

_____

_____

_____

_____

_____

_____

_____

_____

_____

_____

_____

_____

_____

DAY 13

He also said, A man had two sons.
Luke 15:11

Luke 15:11 introduces the parable of the prodigal son, a narrative that provides profound insights into fatherhood. This passage reveals the story of a man with two sons who were extremely different in nature. One son demanded his inheritance and squandered it in reckless living, while the other son remained dutifully at home. This story highlights the obligation of fathers to understand and embrace the individuality of each child.

Fatherhood requires a delicate approach where each child is guided and nurtured according to their unique needs and personalities. The father in the parable demonstrates unconditional love and wisdom, responding to each son differently yet with equal compassion. He welcomes the prodigal son back with open arms, celebrating his return without judgment. Simultaneously, he reassures the elder son, acknowledging his loyalty and addressing his feelings of neglect.

This parable teaches fathers the importance of flexibility in parenting. Each child requires a custom-made approach that respects their differences and fosters their growth. By understanding and responding to the distinct needs of each child, fathers can create a supportive environment that nurtures their development and strengthens family bonds. The story of the prodigal son thus serves as a timeless reminder of the complications and rewards of fatherhood.

Prayer – *Lord, help me to reflect on my children individually; giving me the wisdom to father them according to their unique needs. In Jesus' name, Amen.*

Reflection Questions

List the specific traits, characteristics, and needs of each of your children (or your child if you only have one child). How do you embrace and support their individuality?

_____

_____

_____

_____

_____

_____

_____

_____

_____

_____

_____

_____

_____

_____

_____

_____

How can you do more to make sure that each of your children feels equally valued, loved, and supported?

_____

_____

_____

_____

_____

_____

_____

_____

_____

_____

_____

_____

_____

_____

_____

_____

_____

DAY 14

But those who trust in the Lord will renew their strength, they will soar on wings like eagles, they will run and not become weary, they will walk and not faint.
Isaiah 40:31

Fatherhood is not for the faint of heart. It is a 24/7 commitment that stresses focus and faithfulness. As a father, you may often wrestle with feelings of inadequacy, being underappreciated, and unrecognized. In those moments, remember that you are more than adequate, deeply appreciated, and highly valued. It's important not to dwell on these challenging emotions because our role as fathers is not about seeking accolades or competing with mothers. God knew exactly what He was doing when He chose you to be a father.

Fatherhood requires a profound trust in the Lord. Our guidance and direction come from God. Isaiah 40:31 reminds us that those who trust in the Lord will renew their strength. God provides fathers who trust in Him with the necessary strength for the journey and the endurance for the ups and downs of fatherhood. Embrace this divine support, knowing that your efforts are seen and honored by God.

Let Isaiah's words encourage you: as you place your hope in the Lord, you will find renewed strength to soar on wings like eagles, to run without growing weary, and to walk without fainting. Trust in God's provision and continue to lead your family with faith and determination.

Prayer – *God, I thank you that in the times I feel weary, inadequate, and underappreciated, you renew my strength. I trust you with my feelings. In Jesus' name, Amen.*

Reflection Questions

List your feelings of inadequacy, under appreciation, and being unrecognized as a father. List any other feelings you have in these areas. How do you manage these feelings?

_____

_____

_____

_____

_____

_____

_____

_____

_____

_____

_____

_____

_____

_____

_____

_____

Reflect on this scripture in Isaiah 40:31 by repeating it at least 10 times, trying to commit it to memory. Allow God's word to encourage you during the times you experience the feelings you reflected on. Trust God with your feelings, looking for God to renew your strength as a father. Write any reflections.

_____

_____

_____

_____

_____

_____

_____

_____

_____

_____

_____

_____

_____

_____

DAY 15

Finally, be strengthened by the Lord and by his vast strength. Put on the full armor of God so that you can stand against the schemes of the devil.
Ephesians 6:10-11

Fatherhood is not a sprint; it is a marathon. Once a father, always a father. The road is filled with joys and sorrows, traps and temptations. It is definitely a battle, so it is necessary that we prepare ourselves daily for this life. This verse asks us believers to prepare for battle by equipping ourselves with the spiritual armor of God because our enemy, the Devil, seeks to destroy us. This armor is for us to be able to stand firm and resist the enemy, regardless of the circumstances of fatherhood.

Fathers, standing firm sometimes means we will stand alone, with no appreciation for the responsibility we have been called to, yet I encourage you to stand firm anyway. This is why we need to be strengthened by the Lord and his vast strength. Always remember where your strength comes from. It comes from the Lord your God. The strength to work so you can provide for your children/family; the strength to encourage your children; the strength to be compassionate and show mercy toward them; the strength to discipline them when needed; the strength to love them. It all comes from the Lord. We must ground ourselves in this understanding and seek God with our whole hearts, relying wholeheartedly on Him, so we can stand against the schemes of the devil.

Prayer – God, in the moments along my journey of fatherhood when I have to stand firm, I will rely on you for your strength and power. Please give me the determination to be strengthened by you and you alone. In Jesus' name, Amen.

Reflection Questions

How will you prepare daily for your specific challenges of fatherhood?

_____

_____

_____

_____

_____

_____

_____

_____

_____

_____

_____

_____

_____

_____

_____

_____

Meditate on Ephesians 6:10-20, and as you meditate, reflect on what it looks like, standing strong in the Lord. This reflection will be your reminder of where your strength comes from.

_____

_____

_____

_____

_____

_____

_____

_____

_____

_____

_____

_____

_____

_____

_____

_____

_____

DAY 16

But Jesus overheard them and said to Jairus, "Don't be afraid. Just have faith."
Mark 5:36

This scripture verse reflects on a father named Jairus, who faced a tragic situation in his fatherhood journey when his daughter fell deathly ill. As fathers, our faith will often be tested, especially when we desire to walk with Christ and have Christ lead us in fatherhood. However, as you face your own challenges with your faith and fatherhood, take heart in Jesus' words and find encouragement in this season, "Don't be afraid. Just have faith." This reminds us that it is critical for us to hold on to our faith, especially when everything around us tells us otherwise. Jairus' daughter was very important to him, and his faith was so important to this journey for him as a father. As we guide our children in their daily challenges, we lean on Jairus' example in his time of despair, as he went to Jesus for help—help for his daughter and help for his faith.

Imagine his fear, disappointment, and doubt as Jesus delayed dealing with his concern while He dealt with the woman with the issue of blood. However, what we learn in fatherhood is that regardless of our struggles, we must trust evermore deeply in our Christ because it will serve to be transformational in our fatherhood journey.

Just a reminder, our faith is in the person of Jesus Christ! Be encouraged that no matter what you are facing, trust God anyway!

Prayer – *Lord, in my seasons of desperation, please strengthen my faith in your Son, Jesus Christ, trusting that you are able to help me in these seasons of my life and in the lives of my children. In Jesus' name, Amen.*

Reflection Questions

List any fears, doubts, or disappointments you are feeling as a father.

_____

_____

_____

_____

_____

_____

_____

_____

_____

_____

_____

_____

_____

_____

_____

_____

_____

_____

How can Jairus inspire you to seek the help of Jesus and maintain faith in difficult seasons as a father?

_____

_____

_____

_____

_____

_____

_____

_____

_____

_____

_____

_____

_____

_____

_____

_____

DAY 17

Though an army deploys against me, my heart will not be afraid; though a war breaks out against me, I will still be confident
Psalm 27:3

In this verse, we are shown that to have confidence means to have complete trust or reliability in a person or thing. Confidence requires a state of being certain that the particular course of action is the most effective. This is something we must maintain as fathers, our confidence. I am not suggesting that we, as fathers, know everything and are perfect fathers. However, we must be confident in the God that we serve and rely on the fact that God will help us in our failures and struggles as fathers.

The writer of this psalm expresses that he can face relentless attacks while being surrounded by armies without fear. As a father, I have often been fearful of my ability to fulfill my responsibilities to my children as I faced the pressure of finances, my relationship with my wife, sickness, my career, and my own personal wants and needs. What I have learned is that these pressures can be managed without fear because God is my ultimate protector and sustainer. When we push ourselves to trust God, moving through this road of fatherhood, God shows us that He is the One working things out for us and His glory. This gives us confidence in the present and future, that God will continue to do this, building our confidence in Him, even more.

Prayer – *God, help me to see that You have always been my protector and sustainer. Give me the confidence that I need in You as I face my present and future. In Jesus' name, Amen.*

Reflection Questions

Fathers, what areas of your life do you feel the most pressure? How have you coped with them?

_____

_____

_____

_____

_____

_____

_____

_____

_____

_____

_____

_____

_____

_____

_____

_____

_____

_____

Develop an intentional plan of cultivating and maintaining a sense of confidence in God's protection that you will demonstrate in their presence.

_____

_____

_____

_____

_____

_____

_____

_____

_____

_____

_____

_____

_____

_____

_____

_____

_____

DAY 18

But he said to me, "My grace is sufficient for you,
for my power is perfected in weakness."
2 Corinthians 12:9

As a father, I often struggle with the pressure of having all the answers when it comes to my children and family. My desire in fatherhood is to be able to guide my children with the correct solution in every circumstance. For me, this is strength in fatherhood, knowing the answers and knowing how to get everything done. I have learned, though, that in our moments of weakness, the grace of God shines brighter.

God is and has always been incredibly kind to us as fathers. This is the meaning of "grace." God was gracious to bless us with the children we have. As we confront the challenges on our road of fatherhood—feelings of inadequacy, emotional instability as we deal with our own trauma in life, feelings of not being appreciated or being mistreated—may we remember that moments like these are when the strength of God is most evident in our life. Let us give ourselves permission to release the image of appearing strong but lean into the perfect strength that comes only from God. As we embrace our weakness, we create space for God to be strong! God will not compete with our strength. Only when we allow ourselves to be weak will God be strong in us and for us and make us into the fathers we have been destined to become.

Prayer – Lord, my prayer today is that I release all my desires to maintain the worldly image of strength and allow space to be weak, completely relying on you, God, for the true strength that I need. In Jesus' Name, Amen.

Reflection Questions

Think of a time when God's grace was evident in your life during a moment of weakness. Did this change your perspective of what strength means?

_____

_____

_____

_____

_____

_____

_____

_____

_____

_____

_____

_____

_____

_____

_____

What are you doing to rely more on God's grace and less on your own perceived strength?

_____

_____

_____

_____

_____

_____

_____

_____

_____

_____

_____

_____

_____

_____

_____

_____

_____

_____

DAY 19

So He said to them, "This kind can come out by nothing but prayer and fasting."
Mark 9:29 New King James Version

Here is a frustration with fatherhood. There will be times when you will not be able to help your children at all. No matter your attempts, your resources, your intervention, or anything you have access to, there will still be occasions where nothing you try to do will help. It is during these times that you will be left to embrace the pain of knowing there is nothing in your power you can do for them. However, there is something else you can do—pray and fast. In this text, this father painfully embraces the fact that neither he nor the disciples can help his son because of a spirit that torments him. So, the father brings the matter to Jesus. Jesus then commands the spirit to come out of the son and to never enter him again. Later, the disciples asked why they were unable to drive out the spirit, and Jesus replied that there were times when prayer was the only answer.

Fathers, it is critical for you to pray all the time for your children. Also, fasting is a discipline that we sometimes lack in our lives. In those serious matters in your children's lives, add fasting to your prayers and watch how God moves, working everything out!

Prayer – *God, I ask that you help me to implement fasting as a spiritual discipline in my life. I hear you calling me to fast as I bring matters before you in the lives of my children. Thank you, Lord. In Jesus' name, Amen.*

Reflection Questions

What are some areas of frustration as a father that you realize now there is nothing you can do to change the circumstance? How are you handling this?

_____

_____

_____

_____

_____

_____

_____

_____

_____

_____

_____

_____

_____

_____

What specific circumstances or struggles in your children's lives will you begin to commit to bringing to God, specifically through prayer and fasting? Write out how often you will begin to fast (monthly, weekly, etc.).

_____

_____

_____

_____

_____

_____

_____

_____

_____

_____

_____

_____

_____

_____

_____

_____

DAY 20

We know that all things work together for the good of those who love God, who are called according to his purpose
Romans 8:28

One of the things about being a father is the delayed fruits of your presence in the lives of your children and your efforts to be the best father possible for our children. We may not always see the immediate results that come from our direction, love, and commitment. However, this text reminds us that God is working all things together for good, and our calling as fathers is a part of God's plan for our children. Understand that our prayers, our fasting, our instruction, and every moment we spend guiding our children will contribute to their growth, development, and spiritual formation. Our ultimate goal is for our children to grow up knowing God through His Son, Jesus, and to fulfill the potential that God has for them. With this as our goal, everything we do is worth our efforts.

Fathers, you are instruments that God will use to direct our children toward a life of faith. This journey is long and challenging, but take comfort in knowing that our willingness to fulfill this role will not be in vain. We are planting seeds in our children that will bear fruit in God's timing.

Prayer – *Lord, I thank you for the confidence you have given me in knowing that you are working all things out. I also thank you for allowing me to participate in developing my children into the men and women you are calling them to become. In Jesus' name, Amen.*

Reflection Questions

What motivates you as a father when you do not see the immediate results of your efforts? How can you share those things with other fathers in your community?

_____

_____

_____

_____

_____

_____

_____

_____

_____

_____

_____

_____

_____

_____

_____

Pray over the lives of your children. Ask God to use you as an instrument to continue to guide your children so that God's purpose will manifest in their lives.

_____

_____

_____

_____

_____

_____

_____

_____

_____

_____

_____

_____

_____

_____

_____

DAY 21

Therefore, we do not give up. Even though our outer person is being destroyed, our inner person is being renewed day by day.
2 Corinthians 4:16

Fatherhood is a lifetime journey, and there will be many seasons when you feel exhausted from the responsibility and tempted to redirect your attention solely to yourself. In these seasons, please remember that your children need you to be faithfully present in their lives. Understanding that every fatherly relationship is different, it is crucial that we are faithful to this calling. In other words, no matter what, do not give up.

Resilience and daily commitment to reset and renew your spirit are attributes that fatherhood demands. Do not give up. Outwardly, we may feel worn down by the trials and troubles of life, but inwardly, God is renewing you each day. In Greek, the word "renew" is anakainosis, and it translates to causing something to be new and different, describing a continual renewal. This continual renewal actually strengthens us within and turns our challenges into opportunities for growth. Understand that the difficulties of fatherhood are not working against you; they are working for you. Every struggle will reset and renew you, preparing you to be a better father each day. So never give up, for your unwavering faithfulness is foundational for your children's security and growth, regardless of their age.

Prayer – *Lord, renew my strength today, to be the father for my child that you have called me to be. Give me resilience not to give up. Thank you for being my example of fatherhood. In Jesus' name, Amen.*

Reflection Questions

Reflect on times when you felt like giving up. What was it that kept you pushing forward?

_____

_____

_____

_____

_____

_____

_____

_____

_____

_____

_____

_____

_____

_____

Develop a practice that you can use to build your resilience and commitment as a father during tough times.

_____

_____

_____

_____

_____

_____

_____

_____

_____

_____

_____

_____

_____

_____

_____

_____

_____

Final Reflection

Thank you for taking the time to go through this 21-day devotional for fathers. I hope it has helped you on your journey of fatherhood. I encourage you to reset from time to time, going through this devotional at different periods of your life. If this devotion blessed you, please share it with other fathers you believe would benefit from it. Please share any final reflections you have after completing the 21-days.

_____

_____

_____

_____

_____

_____

_____

_____

_____

_____

_____

Acknowledgements

To my wife, Rochelle. Thank you for your constant love, support in encouragement in my work. To my children, Jeremiah Zachary and Madison. You are my motivation every day and you inspired this writing. To my Dad, Mom, sister and brother. You provided the foundation for me, and I still stand on your shoulders.

To my wonderful members (present and past), thank you for loving me as your pastor. You have shaped me into the pastor that I am today.

To each father who has completed this 21-day journey, thank you! I pray that you are a better father today than you were yesterday, and that daily improvement continues. Continue to RESET, growing stronger each day.

Made in the USA
Las Vegas, NV
09 August 2024

93608768R00056